Be Better with money

Learning How To Manage Your Financial Mindset

Winnie Q

YVNIX PUBLISHING

DISCLAIMER

The information in this book is for informational purposes only and is not intended as financial or legal advice. Consult with a professional before making any financial decisions. The publisher and author make no guarantees regarding the outcomes of using this content. Investment decisions should be made after consulting with a financial advisor and conducting personal research. The publisher and author disclaim any liability for inaccuracies or losses resulting from the information in this book. This content does not establish an advisor-client or attorney-client relationship, and is provided on an "as is" basis. Use at your own risk.

THank you

Thank you to my husband who continues to support and encourage me with each and every endeavor. Nothing I do is possible without you.

"The art is not in making money,
but in keeping it."

- Proverb

contents

Introduction

Mindset

In a world filled with financial challenges and dreams, we often seek lasting financial stability, security, and the promise of abundance. However, our path to financial well-being is not solely about amassing wealth; it includes the realms of mindset, perception, and the nature of prosperity.

At the core of our financial journey is our mindset—a powerful and often underestimated force that shapes our relationship with money and the world at large. Our mindset serves as the filter through which we view and engage with the complexities of financial management. It influences our choices, habits, and, ultimately, our financial path.

A mindset, in the context of our financial exploration, is your unique perspective and approach to money. It forms the bedrock of your financial success. For example, a limiting mindset can lead to worries about financial stability, while an empowering mindset can nurture confidence and growth. Your mindset guides your decision-making, goal-setting, and navigation of the financial landscapes in your life.

Let's illustrate this with a scenario:

Limiting Mindset: "I don't have enough time to complete this project. I'm overwhelmed and stressed."

Empowering Mindset: "I have the time and resources to complete this project effectively. I will manage my time better and be more organized."

Our mindset significantly impacts our perception of time, which brings us to the second facet of our journey: understanding that money, in essence, represents time.

The Currency of Time

Money, it turns out, is the currency that measures the time we spend working for it. When we purchase an item or invest in an experience, we are essentially exchanging our time, our life force, for that value. This shift in perspective—from viewing money as mere currency to recognizing it as a precious and limited resource—invites us to reevaluate our financial choices. It asks us to consider how wisely we invest our time in exchange for the things that matter most.

Consider this: You have your eyes set on a brand-new big-screen TV. It's got all the bells and whistles, and the price tag reads $1500. Now, think about your job; you earn $15 per hour. If you were to buy that TV, it would cost you a substantial 100 hours of work. When you look at it this way, you're not just paying $1500; you're trading 100 hours of your life for that television. Suddenly, the value of your time becomes strikingly apparent, making you contemplate whether that purchase is worth the significant investment of your life's hours.

Objective

With these fundamental principles in mind the objective of this book is to guide you in the way you perceive and interact with financial matters as well as provide you with practical applications and strategies that empower you to be better with money. In the chapters ahead, we'll strike a balance between mindset and practicality.

WARNING!

In this journey towards financial empowerment, you may notice several recurring themes and ideas throughout the chapters. This repetition isn't by chance; it's a deliberate and purposeful approach. Think of it like this: when you were learning to ride a bike, it wasn't a one-time event. You needed consistent practice to build the muscle memory and coordination required to balance on two wheels. The same principle applies here. Repetition is our way of reinforcing essential financial concepts, like budgeting, saving, and investing, until they become second nature. We believe that true transformation occurs through consistent practice and application. So, don't be surprised if you encounter familiar ideas across these pages – each repetition is a step towards changing your mindset and, ultimately, your financial life.

CHAPTER ONE

YOUR MONEY MINDSET

When it comes to finances, your personal mindset is pivotal. It shapes your thoughts, beliefs, and, ultimately, your financial reality. Think of your mind as a steering wheel. Just as a driver directs a vehicle, you guide your thoughts about money, which then steer your financial beliefs. Your money mindset, like a steering wheel, determines the direction you take and what you leave behind.

You may have encountered bumps and detours on your financial journey, but remember, it's not about the road you've traveled; it's about the direction you choose moving forward. Much like a GPS recalibrates your route when you take a wrong turn, you can recalibrate your mindset to chart a course for financial success. By practicing awareness and embracing empowering ideas, you can navigate toward abundance, making your financial goals a reality.

Learned Mindset

You must first understand your relationship with money. From a young age, we absorb various messages about money, much like how an artist learns different techniques and styles. These early lessons are often painted by the influences around us, primarily our parents or guardians. Their beliefs, habits, and attitudes about money leave indelible marks on us.

Just as an artist selects a palette of colors to create their masterpiece, we develop a palette of financial beliefs. These beliefs are like the hues an artist uses to paint the scenes of their life. They dictate our financial choices, impacting everything from our spending habits to our long-term financial goals.

As we navigate life, our beliefs about money manifest in the choices we make. Just as an artist's canvas reveals their vision, our financial reality reflects the ideas and attitudes we've acquired. It's not merely about brushing strokes onto the canvas; it's about understanding the colors we choose and the meaning they bring to our financial masterpiece.

Examples:

Savings and Investment: If your parents instilled a strong belief in saving and investing for the future, you are likely to prioritize building an emergency fund and contributing to retirement accounts. This mindset leads to the practical choice of allocating a portion of your income to savings and investments.

Lack of Financial Planning: Growing up in an environment where financial planning was neglected can result in neglecting to create your own financial plan. This might lead to missed opportunities to save and invest, ultimately hindering your long-term financial well-being.

Spending Habits: Growing up in a household where frugality was emphasized may lead to a preference for budget-conscious decisions. You might choose to shop for discounts, avoid unnecessary expenses, and prioritize needs over wants.

Impulse Spending: If your parents had a tendency to make impulsive and unplanned purchases, you might find yourself repeating this pattern. This can lead to accumulating credit card debt due to unplanned and unnecessary expenditures.

These are just a few examples of how the mindset acquired from parents can shape financial choices. Our early financial education, whether consciously or unconsciously absorbed, often becomes a powerful determinant in our adult financial behavior. Recognizing these influences is the first step in making mindful financial choices and, if needed, in adapting or reshaping your financial mindset.

Cultivating Empowerment

The encouraging truth is that your money mindset is adaptable. It's not a fixed trait but a perspective you can actively shape. Start by recognizing any negative beliefs about money that may be limiting you. Acknowledge those thoughts without passing judgment. In doing so, you open the door to transformation. You can shift your perspective by recognizing and replacing limiting beliefs with empowering ones, effectively rewriting your financial story for a brighter future.

Examples:

Limiting Money Belief: "I don't need a budget; I can handle my finances on the fly."
Empowering Idea: "Creating and sticking to a budget helps me manage my money effectively and plan for the future."

Limiting Money Belief: "I don't need to save; I'll figure it out later."
Empowering Idea: "Regular savings allow me to build a financial safety net and work toward my financial goals."

Practical Steps

Building a strong financial foundation begins with the right mindset. These practical steps are essential in fostering a positive financial outlook:

1. **Daily Affirmations of Gratitude**: Start each day with positive affirmations about what you do have and what your money is providing.

2. **Track Your Spending**: Keep a detailed record of your expenses for a month. This will help you understand where exactly your money is going. (We will use this next chapter)

3. **Set Specific Financial Goals**: Define measurable goals. Saving for vacation, paying off debt, or building an emergency fund, setting targets gives your a purpose and direction.

Conclusion

Your relationship with money is a reflection of your inner beliefs. It's like a mirror showing how you think and feel about finances. By shifting your financial mindset, you can actively change your financial direction.

CHAPTER TWO

THE FUNDAMENTALS

In any venture, whether you're learning a musical instrument or playing a sport, mastering the fundamentals is crucial for success. Just like a skilled musician who starts with scales or a talented athlete who perfects their basic techniques, in the realm of personal finance, mastering the core principles is equally essential. It's these fundamentals that form the building blocks of financial planning, providing a solid foundation for your monetary strategy. Think of them as the training wheels on your bicycle – they ensure you have the balance and stability needed to navigate life's financial journey with confidence and resilience.

Just as every grand symphony begins with the simplest notes, and every sports champion starts with the basics, your journey to financial success commences with these fundamental principles. In this chapter, we'll explore budgeting, the importance of emergency funds, effective debt management, and the significance of regular savings. These elements serve as your anchors in the ever-changing sea of personal finance, ensuring you're well-equipped to navigate life's uncertainties. So, let's begin with the essentials, for they lay the groundwork for the more advanced concepts and strategies you'll explore in the chapters ahead.

Budgeting: Your Financial Compass

Budgeting is the compass that guides your financial decisions. It's not about restricting your spending; it's about making intentional choices with your money. Start by tracking your expenses for a month to understand where your money goes. Wait, you already did that last chapter during the Practical Steps! This simple act of awareness can be enlightening, helping you better understand where your money goes and nudging you toward more purposeful financial decisions.

- Create a monthly budget: List your sources of income and allocate specific amounts for expenses like housing, food, transportation, and entertainment.

- Monitor your spending: Use an app or spreadsheets to track your expenses regularly. This helps you stay on course.

- Adjust as needed: Be flexible with your budget and adjust it when your circumstances change. Life is dynamic, and your budget should be too.

Example:

Category	Monthly Amount
Income	
Salary	$3,000
Side Gig Income	$500
Total Income	**$3,500**
Expenses	
Housing (Rent/Mortgage)	$1,200
Utilities (Electricity, Water, Gas)	$150
Groceries	$400
Transportation (Car Payment, Gas)	$300
Health Insurance	$100
Entertainment	$100
Dining Out	$100
Savings	$250
Total Expenses	**$2,500**
Remaining	**$1,000**

In this example, the person's total monthly income is $3,500, while their total monthly expenses amount to $2,500, leaving $1,000 as a surplus for savings or other financial goals. This is a basic template, and actual budgets may vary based on individual circumstances and financial objectives.

A well-structured budget forms the solid base of your financial stability. It empowers you to assert control over your finances and make informed decisions.

Emergency Funds: Your Financial Safety Net

Life is unpredictable, and unexpected expenses can arise at any time. An emergency fund is your safety net, providing peace of mind when facing unexpected challenges. Whether it's a sudden medical bill, a car repair, or even a job loss, having a readily accessible financial cushion allows you to tackle these situations without dipping into your regular savings or going into debt. It's your shield against financial stress and an essential part of your overall financial security.

- Set a goal: Aim to save at least three to six months' worth of living expenses in your emergency fund.

- Start small: Begin with a small, manageable goal, like $500. Gradually increase it as you can.

- Automatic savings: Set up automatic transfers to your emergency fund each month, treating it like a non-negotiable bill. *Add it to your budget.*

Managing Debt: Your Path to Freedom

Debt can be a heavy burden, but it's not impossible to overcome. Effectively managing it is a crucial step in reinforcing your financial security. By creating a well-structured debt repayment plan, you regain control over your finances and free up resources for your financial goals. This proactive approach not only reduces the weight of debt but also helps you regain your financial footing, allowing you to build a more stable and prosperous future.

- List your debts: Make a comprehensive list of all your debts, including their interest rates and minimum monthly payments.

- Avoid new debt: While paying off existing debt, minimize taking on new debt whenever possible.

- Create a debt repayment plan: Decide on a strategy, whether it's the snowball method (paying off small debts first) or the avalanche method (tackling high-interest debts first).

Snowball Method

Debt Account	Balance	Minimum Payment	Interest Rate
Credit Card A	$1,500	$50	18%
Personal Loan	$5,000	$150	10%
Medical Bill	$800	$30	0%
Student Loan	$15,000	$200	5%
Car Loan	$8,000	$250	4%
Total	$30,300	$680	-

In the snowball method, you would prioritize paying off the debts from the smallest balance to the largest while continuing to make the minimum payments on all other debts. After eliminating the first debt, you would apply the freed-up money to the next smallest debt and continue the process until you are debt-free. This method is effective for building momentum and motivation as you see smaller debts being paid off.

Avalanche Method

Debt Account	Balance	Minimum Payment	Interest Rate
Credit Card A	$1,500	$50	18%
Student Loan	$15,000	$200	6%
Car Loan	$8,000	$250	4.5%
Personal Loan	$5,000	$150	4%
Medical Bill	$800	$30	0%
Total	$30,300	$680	-

In the avalanche method, you would prioritize paying off the debts with the highest interest rates first while continuing to make the minimum payments on all other debts. After eliminating the first high-interest debt, you would apply the freed-up money to the next highest-interest debt and continue the process until you are debt-free. This method is effective for minimizing the total interest paid over time.

Savings: Your Future Self's Best Friend

Savings lay the groundwork for a prosperous future, equipping you to reach your objectives with confidence. They provide the means to achieve your long-term goals, whether it's buying a home, funding your child's education, or securing a comfortable retirement. Having a robust savings strategy in place ensures that you're financially prepared for life's milestones and unexpected expenses.

- <u>Set specific savings goals</u>: Whether it's for a vacation, a home, or retirement, define your objectives.

- <u>Pay yourself first</u>: Prioritize saving by setting up automatic transfers to your savings accounts. *Add it to your budget.*

- <u>Diversify your savings</u>: Consider different accounts for short-term and long-term goals, like a high-yield savings account and retirement accounts.

Practical Steps

Creating a strong financial footing involves mastering these fundamental elements: budgeting, emergency funds, managing debt, and savings. Here are some ways to help you implement these ideas.

1. **Budgeting**: Create a monthly budget, monitor your spending, and adjust as needed.

2. **Emergency Funds**: Set a goal to save at least three to six months' worth of living expenses. Start small, automate savings, and prioritize this fund.

3. **Managing Debt**: List your debts, create a debt repayment plan, and avoid new debt.

4. **Savings**: Set specific savings goals, pay yourself first, and diversify your savings.

Conclusion

These fundamentals provide not only a roadmap but also the tools needed to navigate the complexities of personal finance. They empower you to take control of your financial destiny and make informed choices, creating a strong financial footing for whatever life may bring your way. By mastering these key elements, you're not only ensuring stability but also setting the stage for prosperity and financial security, granting you the freedom to pursue your dreams and achieve lasting financial well-being.

Chapter Three

ASSETS VS STUFF

Welcome, dear readers, to the intriguing world of assets and stuff. In this chapter, we'll embark on a journey to distinguish between what's truly valuable and what merely fills our closets. As we explore this concept, let's not forget the sage wisdom of the song "If I Had a Million Dollars" by the Barenaked Ladies.

"I'd buy you a green dress, but not a real green dress, that's cruel." Indeed, the line encapsulates a profound truth – a dress, no matter how stylish or lack there of, is not an asset.

The Green Dress Conundrum

Imagine a scenario where you have a million dollars at your disposal. You could spend it on a myriad of things, including that coveted green dress. However, the green dress would not enhance your financial well-being in the long run. In fact, it might depreciate in value the moment you walk out of the store.

This is the essence of the assets vs. stuff dilemma. Assets are the greenback equivalents of financial instruments, investments, and properties – the things that grow and multiply your wealth. Stuff, on the other hand, encompasses all the tangible possessions that often lose value over time – like that not so beautiful and fleeting green dress.

Assets: The Money Multipliers

Assets are the money multipliers in your financial universe. They are the investments that have the potential to appreciate, gaining value over time, and thereby generating wealth and prosperity. By strategically growing your assets, you create opportunities for long-term financial growth and the ability to secure your financial future. Let's look at a few key asset categories:

- <u>Stocks and Bonds</u>: Investing in stocks and bonds allows your money to work for you. Over time, these investments can yield dividends, interest, and capital gains, all contributing to your financial growth.

- <u>Real Estate</u>: Owning property can be a powerful asset. As property values increase, your net worth grows. Additionally, rental income can provide a steady stream of cash flow.

- <u>Business Ventures</u>: Entrepreneurship and investments in businesses have the potential for substantial returns. A successful business can be one of your most valuable assets.

- <u>Retirement Accounts</u>: Contributing to retirement accounts like a 401(k) or an IRA is akin to planting seeds for your financial future. These accounts can appreciate over time, helping you secure a comfortable retirement.

Stuff: The Fleeting Pleasures and Deceptive Delights

Stuff, while enjoyable and sometimes necessary, often has a short shelf life when it comes to its financial value. That green dress you bought today may not hold the same allure a year from now, and its resale value is unlikely to bring a return on your investment. However, there's a twist to the stuff saga – some possessions may cleverly masquerade as assets when, in fact, they are simply stuff in disguise.

Deceptive Delights

Luxury Cars: While owning a luxury car can be a status symbol, it's usually a depreciating asset. It may give you comfort and prestige, but it won't increase in value over time.

Electronics and Gadgets: The latest smartphone or gaming console can be tempting, but technology evolves rapidly, and these items quickly lose value as newer models emerge.

Collectibles and Memorabilia: Items like sports memorabilia or collectible toys can be exciting to own, but their value is often tied to trends and fads, making it uncertain whether they will appreciate over time.

Home Renovations: Extensive renovations to your home may improve its comfort and aesthetics, but they may not always provide a dollar-for-dollar return on investment when you sell the property.

Practical Steps

Let's look at some tips that can help you can gain clarity on the distinction between assets and stuff, make more thoughtful purchase decisions, and align your spending with your financial objectives.

1. **Create a List of Needs vs. Wants:** Before making any purchase, categorize the item as a need or a want. Needs are essential for daily living, like groceries, while wants are non-essential items, like a new gadget. This simple classification helps you differentiate between necessary expenses and discretionary spending.

2. **Set a Price-to-Value Ratio**: Assign a price-to-value ratio to your purchases. For example, for non-essential items, you might decide that an item should provide value equivalent to its price. This means it should enhance your life or bring joy in proportion to the cost. This practice encourages you to weigh the true worth of what you're buying.

   Reminder: Money is the time we spend working for it. You can also measure the value of the item by how many hours it will take you to work to pay for it.

3. **The "30-Day Rule"**: When considering a non-essential purchase, wait for at least 30 days before buying it. During this period, assess whether you still want or

need the item. This waiting period can help reduce impulsive buying and ensure your purchases align with your long-term financial goals.

Step	Action	Explanation
1	Identify the Purchase	When you feel the urge to make an impulse purchase, take note of the item or experience you desire.
2	Wait for 30 Days	Commit to delaying the purchase for a full 30 days. This waiting period allows you to assess whether the desire is fleeting or something you genuinely want or need.
3	Make a Note	During the 30-day waiting period, jot down the details of the item or experience you're considering buying. Include its cost, purpose, and why you want it.
4	Research Alternatives	Investigate if there are more cost-effective options or alternatives to the purchase.
5	Reevaluate	After 30 days, revisit your notes and the item or experience you wanted to buy. Ask yourself if it still holds the same appeal.
6	Budget or Save	If the item or experience remains a priority and aligns with your financial goals, incorporate it into your budget or savings plan. This step ensures that impulse purchases are made consciously and within your financial plan.

Conclusion

We've explored how assets, with their potential for appreciation and wealth generation, server as the true engines of financial prosperity. These principles offer not only a clear understanding but also practical tools for discerning the financial choices that will shape your future. By recognizing and prioritizing assets over mere possessions, you're not only creating a roadmap to success but also equipping yourself with the tools to build lasting wealth and security.

TIME OUT : REFLECT & REALIGN

Kudos on exploring the core principles and grasping the interplay between assets and material possessions. As we move forward, let's pause for a moment of contemplation and self-evaluation. Your understanding of these core concepts is essential, but it's equally crucial to examine how they shape your financial choices and lifestyle. This Time Out provides a chance to check your mindset, reevaluate your financial goals, and confirm that you're making the right strides toward wealth and financial security.

Reassess Your Financial Goals

Take a moment to revisit your financial goals. Are they still in alignment with your aspirations? Have they evolved since you started this journey? Adjust and refine them as necessary.

Evaluate Your Money Mindset

Consider your beliefs and thoughts about money. Are there any limiting beliefs that you've identified during your study of the fundamentals? How can you shift your mindset to be more aligned with abundance and financial success?

Examine Your Spending Habits

Reflect on your spending habits. Are there areas where you can cut back to save more for your financial goals? What changes can you implement to ensure your spending aligns with your aspirations?

Assess Your Current Assets

Examine your current assets and investments. Are there any adjustments or diversifications needed to optimize your portfolio? How do these assets fit into your long-term wealth-building strategy?

Revisit Your Financial Plan

Revisit your financial plan to ensure it accommodates the insights gained from the previous chapters. Does it need modifications based on the fundamentals you've learned? Make the necessary adjustments to ensure your plan remains on track.

CELEBRATE YOUR PROGRESS

Take a moment to recognize the progress you've made on your path to financial success, even if it's as simple as your commitment to learning through this book.

"It is not the strongest of the species that survive, nor the most intelligent, but the one most responsive to change."

Charles Darwin

This Time Out section serves as a checkpoint, an opportunity to reassess, realign, and refocus on your financial aspirations. Feel free to jot down your reflections and make any adjustments to your financial strategies as needed. As we proceed, remember that your growth and success are rooted in consistent reflection and action.

Chapter Four

REAL ESTATE & WEALTH BUILDING

Historically, real estate has been a dependable avenue toward prosperity. It combines stability, appreciation potential, and avenues for passive income generation. Yet, it comes with its share of challenges, making it essential to approach with a well-informed strategy.

It's important to understand that success often hinges on thorough research, careful planning, and effective execution. The real estate market is ever-evolving, which means the best strategies today may differ from those of tomorrow. However, by developing a deep understanding of the market, staying updated on the latest trends, and employing effective property management and investment practices, you can navigate the challenges and pave your way towards financial prosperity.

The Investment Opportunities

Opportunities for investment are as diverse as the properties themselves. You can explore residential real estate, commercial real estate, or even specialized niches like industrial properties or multifamily units. Each avenue has its unique potential for growth and profitability. For instance, residential real estate often provides a steady stream of rental income, while commercial properties offer the opportunity to secure long-term leases with businesses. Depending on your financial goals and risk tolerance, you can choose to invest in properties that require minimal renovations or those with substantial value-add potential.

As with any investment, there are inherent risks involved in real estate, such as market fluctuations, property management challenges, and financing complexities. That's why it's crucial to conduct thorough market research, develop a sound investment strategy, and, if needed, seek professional guidance. By analyzing the local real estate market and understanding your investment objectives, you can make informed decisions on which properties to invest in, how to finance your investments, and how to optimize your portfolio for long-term success. The key to successful real estate investment lies in diversification, careful risk management, and a deep understanding of your chosen market.

Examples:

- <u>Homeownership</u>: Owning your own home is often the first step in real estate investment. While your primary residence may not provide immediate financial returns, it can be a valuable asset over time.

- <u>Rental Properties</u>: Investing in rental properties can generate consistent cash flow through monthly rent payments. Over the long term, rental properties can appreciate in value, making them an excellent wealth-building tool.

- <u>Real Estate Investment Trusts (REITs)</u>: REITs allow you to invest in real estate without the need for direct ownership. They offer dividends and the potential for capital appreciation.

Location, Location, Location

The significance of location in real estate cannot be overstated. Consider this: two identical houses, one situated in a quiet, family-friendly neighborhood with excellent schools, parks, and shopping centers within walking distance, and the other in an area far from these amenities. The former, thanks to its convenient location, can command higher rents and experience more significant appreciation in value over time. The latter, lacking these advantages, may struggle to attract tenants and experience limited growth in value.

Location can also be a determining factor when it comes to the resilience of your real estate investment in the face of economic downturns. Properties in prime locations tend to remain in demand, even during economic challenges, providing more stability for your investment. Moreover, a property in a desirable location can potentially serve as a more robust source of rental income. For investors, making location-based decisions involves conducting thorough market research, assessing the neighborhood's growth potential, and staying updated on local trends. A well-located property can be your ticket to a thriving real estate investment.

Practical Steps

As we navigate the landscape of real estate, it's essential to be equipped with practical strategies to make informed property decisions. Preparation and informed decision-making is where you wealth through property begins. These practical steps serve as your compass, guiding you toward sound real estate choices that can help you build wealth and secure your financial future.

1. **Research Local Market**: Understand your local real estate market, property values, and rental demand.

2. **Financial Planning**: Assess your budget and determine how much you can invest in real estate.

3. **Expert Advice**: Consider consulting real estate professionals for guidance.

Conclusion

Real estate can be a powerful wealth-building tool, offering the potential for appreciation and passive income. However, it's not without its challenges, so it's crucial to approach it with knowledge and a clear financial plan. By understanding the local market and creating a plan, you can harness the potential of real estate to bolster your financial future.

It offers opportunities that extend beyond the mere purchase of a property. It allows you to engage with your financial resources actively and strategically, resulting in a thriving financial portfolio. As you journey into the real estate market, remember that it's not just about owning properties; it's about making informed decisions, managing assets effectively, and growing your wealth.

CHAPTER FIVE

INVESTMENT STRATEGIES

Investments are where your money has the power to flourish and pave the way for a more prosperous future. There are various investment strategies, each designed to assist you in building and nurturing your wealth over time. There is a diverse range of financial instruments, each offering distinct avenues to enhance your financial growth and establish a secure foundation for the life you aspire to lead.

The Power of Investing

Investing is a pivotal force in wealth building because it empowers your money to work for you. Rather than idly storing your savings, investments offer the exciting potential for both growth and income. The act of investing, in essence, is like planting seeds that can flourish into trees bearing fruits of financial success.

However, it's crucial to acknowledge that investing comes with its fair share of risks and uncertainties. To navigate these waters successfully, one must be armed with not only financial knowledge but also a carefully crafted strategy. Knowledge allows you to make informed decisions about which investment opportunities align with your financial goals, while a well-thought-out strategy provides you with a clear roadmap to guide your investment choices. Together, knowledge and strategy are your most potent allies when embarking on the exciting journey of investing.

Diversification: The Key to Risk Management

Diversification serves as a fundamental principle in investing, akin to the age-old wisdom of not putting all your eggs in one basket. It entails distributing your investments among various asset classes, including stocks, bonds, real estate, and more. By doing so, you mitigate risk by lessening the potential negative impact of underperforming assets within a single class on your entire portfolio.

Just as having multiple baskets prevents the loss of all your eggs with a single mishap, diversification safeguards your investments from significant losses in a single asset class, providing a cushion for your overall financial strategy. This approach helps balance the potential for growth while minimizing exposure to adverse market fluctuations, contributing to the resilience of your investment portfolio.

Investment Vehicles

Investment vehicles are the tools and mechanisms that allow you to participate in the world of investing. These encompass a wide array of options, each with its unique characteristics and potential benefits. Whether you're looking for safety, income, growth, or a combination of these, there's an investment vehicle suitable for your goals

Each of these vehicles comes with its unique set of risks and rewards, offering opportunities for diversification and the potential to enhance your wealth over time. As you explore your options, it's crucial to align your choices with your financial objectives, risk tolerance, and investment horizon to build a well-rounded and effective investment portfolio.

- <u>Stocks</u>: Investing in stocks means buying shares of ownership in a company. Stocks offer the potential for capital appreciation and dividends but come with higher volatility.

- <u>Bonds</u>: Bonds are debt securities issued by governments or corporations. They provide regular interest payments and return the principal amount at maturity. Bonds are generally considered lower risk than stocks.

- <u>Mutual Funds and Exchange Traded Funds (ETFs)</u>: These pool money from multiple investors to buy a diversified portfolio of stocks, bonds, or other assets.

In addition to these traditional investment vehicles, the world of investing also includes various alternative options like already mentioned real estate, peer-to-peer lending, dividend stocks, commodities, cryptocurrencies, and venture capital investments.

This table offers a quick overview of various investment strategies, their pros and cons, and typical returns. Keep in mind that these are general figures and actual returns can vary depending on individual circumstances and market conditions.

Investment Vehicle	Description	Pros	Cons	Typical Returns
Stock Market	Investing in individual stocks or ETFs	Potential for high returns	High volatility	5-10% per year
Real Estate	Buying and holding rental properties	Generates rental income	Requires substantial capital	5-10% per year
Bonds	Investing in government or corporate bonds	Steady, predictable income	Lower returns compared to stocks	2-5% per year
Mutual Funds	Diversified portfolio managed by a fund	Professional management	Management fees	5-7% per year
Peer-to-Peer Lending	Providing loans to individuals or small businesses	Monthly interest payments	Risk of borrower default	3-7% per year
Dividend Stocks	Investing in stocks known for paying dividends	Regular income	Stock price volatility	3-6% per year

Investment Strategies

Investment strategies serve as the roadmaps guiding your decisions within the world of investing. They represent a systematic and well-thought-out approach to achieving your financial goals while managing risk effectively. These strategies encompass a spectrum of approaches, each tailored to address specific objectives, risk tolerances, and investment timelines.

- <u>Buy and Hold</u>: This strategy involves purchasing investments and holding them for the long term, regardless of market fluctuations. It takes advantage of the power of compounding and minimizes trading costs.

- <u>Dollar-Cost Averaging</u>: With this method, you invest a fixed amount of money at regular intervals, regardless of market conditions. It can help reduce the impact of market volatility on your investments.

- <u>Value Investing</u>: Value investors seek stocks or assets they believe are undervalued by the market. They aim to buy low and sell high when the market recognizes the asset's true value.

Active trading strategies are employed by investors who aim to capitalize on short-term market movements. Day trading, swing trading, and other active strategies involve making frequent transactions within shorter timeframes, often leveraging market research and technical analysis. While these strategies offer the potential for quick gains, they also come with a higher degree of risk and typically require a deep understanding of market dynamics. It's essential to align your strategy with your financial goals, risk tolerance, and investment horizon to ensure that it complements your unique financial journey effectively.

Practical Steps

These practical steps offer a comprehensive approach to building and managing an investment strategy that aligns with your financial aspirations and risk profile. They underscore the significance of planning, risk management, and continuous learning to secure your financial future.

1. **Set Clear Investment Goals:** Identifying your financial objectives is essential for crafting an effective investment strategy. Whether you're saving for retirement, a home, or your children's education, knowing your goals helps you define your investment horizon and the level of risk you can undertake.

2. **Assess Your Risk Tolerance**: Understanding your comfort with risk is a crucial step. Your risk tolerance should be compatible with your investment strategy to ensure you don't experience unnecessary anxiety or panic during market fluctuations. This alignment is vital for maintaining a long-term investment outlook.

3. **Diversify Your Portfolio**: Diversification helps mitigate risk by spreading your investments across various asset classes, such as stocks, bonds, real estate, and more. By diversifying, you reduce the impact of poor performance in one asset class on your entire portfolio. Seeking advice from a financial advisor can be particularly valuable in constructing a well-diversified portfolio tailored to your goals and risk tolerance.

4. **Stay Informed**: Keeping up with market trends and economic developments is an ongoing process. The more you know about the investment landscape, the better equipped you are to make informed decisions. Whether through financial news, books, seminars, or the guidance of a trusted advisor, staying informed is a powerful tool in your investment toolkit.

Conclusion

As you set clear investment goals, understand your risk tolerance, diversify your portfolio, and stay informed about market trends, you are taking significant steps towards financial empowerment. It's crucial to keep in mind that investing is not a quick fix, but a path to long-term wealth. The discipline to stick with your strategy, even during market fluctuations, and the patience to watch your investments grow are essential attributes for any successful investor. Remember that the choices you make today will have a profound impact on your financial future, and with the right approach, you can build the wealth and security you aspire to.

The key is to maintain your commitment to learning and adapting your strategies as you progress. Investing can be a fulfilling and rewarding pursuit, and it all starts with the knowledge and strategies you've gained here.

CHAPTER SIX

RETIREMENT PLANNING & WEALTH PRESERVATION

Welcome to the section dedicated to securing your financial future and preserving the wealth you've worked diligently to build. Here, we'll explore the importance of retirement planning and the strategies you can employ to safeguard your financial legacy. This is your guide to ensuring your later years are as prosperous as your active working life.

Retirement planning is not a luxury; it's a necessity. It's the roadmap to ensure that your later years are comfortable and free from financial stress. Whether you dream of traveling the world, pursuing hobbies, or simply enjoying your well-deserved rest, retirement planning is the key.

Retirement Accounts and Options

One essential aspect of retirement planning involves choosing the right options. These financial tools are designed to help you save, invest, and secure your financial future. Consider options like employer-sponsored plans such as 401(k) and 403(b), which offer tax advantages and potential for long-term growth. Additionally, Individual Retirement Accounts (IRAs) like Traditional IRAs and Roth IRAs provide tax benefits for retirement savings. Some employers may offer traditional pensions, guaranteeing regular income, and annuities are another option, allowing you to exchange a lump sum for guaranteed income. Understanding these retirement accounts and options is a crucial step in ensuring a prosperous retirement.

Examples:

- <u>401(k) and 403(b) Plans</u>: These employer-sponsored retirement accounts allow you to contribute a portion of your salary, often with employer matching.

- <u>Individual Retirement Accounts (IRAs)</u>: IRAs provide tax advantages for retirement savings. Traditional IRAs offer tax-deferred growth, while Roth IRAs offer tax-free withdrawals in retirement.

- <u>Pensions and Annuities:</u> Some employers offer traditional pensions, providing regular income in retirement. Annuities are another option, allowing you to exchange a lump sum for guaranteed income.

Long-Term Wealth Preservation Strategies

While accumulating wealth is an impressive achievement, preserving and protecting it over the long haul is equally essential. These strategies are not just about growing your wealth but ensuring that it continues to work for you and your loved ones, even beyond your lifetime.

One key aspect of Long-Term Wealth Preservation is estate planning. This entails creating a comprehensive estate plan that may include a will, trusts, and powers of attorney. By doing so, you can safeguard your assets, ensure they are distributed according to your wishes, and minimize the impact of estate taxes. Your estate plan is not just a legal document; it's a reflection of your financial legacy, providing a blueprint for the transfer of your wealth and assets while mitigating potential financial pitfalls.

Another integral strategy is tax-efficient investing. As part of your long-term wealth preservation plan, consider investment strategies that minimize your tax liability. This may involve holding investments for the long term to benefit from favorable capital gains tax rates or using tax-advantaged accounts. Reducing your tax burden can significantly impact the overall growth and preservation of your wealth. Additionally, don't forget about asset protection, which involves safeguarding your assets from potential creditors or legal challenges. Utilizing legal structures such as trusts and limited liability companies (LLCs) can add an extra layer of protection to your financial legacy, ensuring it remains intact and secure for generations to come.

Examples:

- Estate Planning: Create a comprehensive estate plan that includes a will, trusts, and powers of attorney. This ensures that your assets are distributed according to your wishes and minimizes estate taxes.

- Tax-Efficient Investing: Consider tax-efficient investment strategies to minimize your tax liability, such as holding investments for the long term or using tax-advantaged accounts.

- Asset Protection: Shield your assets from potential creditors or lawsuits through legal structures like trusts and limited liability companies (LLCs).

Practical Steps

As we focus on practical steps of retirement planning and wealth preservation, you're embarking on a journey towards lasting prosperity. These actionable strategies are the great ways of safeguarding your retirement years and securing the legacy.

1. **Consult an Estate Planning Attorney**: Seeking professional legal advice is essential for creating or updating your estate plan. In addition to this step, consider discussing the establishment of trusts and other legal mechanisms that can protect your assets and minimize tax implications. This practical step can ensure your financial legacy is well-preserved..

2. **Review and Adjust**: Regularly assessing your financial plan and investment portfolio is crucial. To expand upon this step, emphasize the importance of staying informed about changes in financial regulations and tax laws, and adapting your plan accordingly. This way, your wealth preservation strategies remain effective over time.

3. **Insurance**: The inclusion of insurance is valuable in mitigating potential financial risks. In addition to life insurance and liability coverage, consider other forms of insurance such as long-term care insurance and disability insurance. Diversifying your insurance coverage can provide comprehensive protection for your wealth.

Conclusion

Retirement planning is what guides you towards financial security in your later years. It's a journey that requires foresight and disciplined savings. By setting clear goals, calculating your retirement needs, making regular contributions, and diversifying your investments, you'll be better equipped to enjoy a fulfilling retirement.

Wealth preservation is not just about safeguarding your assets; it's about ensuring your financial legacy benefits your loved ones and the causes you care about. By engaging in estate planning, optimizing your tax strategy, and exploring asset protection measures, you can create a solid foundation for preserving your wealth for generations to come.

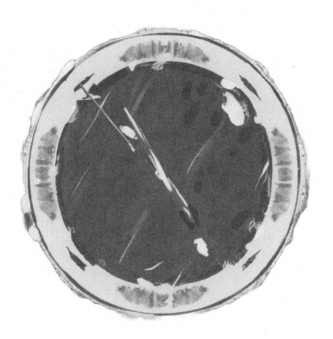

TIME OUT : STOP & THINK

You've explored the world of real estate, ventured into investment strategies, and engaged in retirement planning and wealth preservation. Now that you've ventured into these financial areas, how have your perspectives evolved? Have you encountered new opportunities or challenges that have shifted your approach to managing your wealth?

Remember, it's not just about what you read but how you apply what you learn. Use this moment to realign your financial aspirations, refine your goals, and refocus your energy.

Take a moment to pause and reflect. As you do, consider these questions:

What Excites You?
Reflect on the aspects of real estate, investment, or retirement planning that truly excite you. What motivates you to learn and grow in these areas?

Have You Set Financial Goals?
What are your specific financial goals? Have they evolved during your reading journey? Write down your short-term and long-term objectives.

Mindset Check
Take a moment to assess your mindset. Are there limiting ideas that need adjustment? Are you embracing a wealth-building mindset?

Implementation
What practical steps from the chapters you've covered will you put into practice immediately? How can you apply what you've learned in a tangible way? What practical steps from the chapters you've covered will you put into practice immediately? How can you apply what you've learned in a tangible way?

Learning Continuation
What aspects of real estate, investments, or retirement planning do you want to explore further? Are there specific areas you want to deepen your knowledge in?

CELEBRATE YOUR ACHIEVEMENTS

Pause and celebrate the steps you've taken. Whether it's the newfound knowledge you've acquired or the decisions you've made to secure your financial future.

"Success is not final, failure is not fatal: It is the courage to continue that counts."

- Winston Churchill

CHAPTER SEVEN

PASSIVE INCOME STREAMS & FINANCIAL FREEDOM

Passive income is a potential game-changer. It's money earned with minimal effort or active involvement, enabling you to accumulate wealth while savoring the rewards of your hard work. This income stream can come from various sources, such as rental properties, dividends from investments, royalties, or income generated from a well-established online business. By incorporating passive income into your financial strategy, you create the opportunity to achieve financial security and even free up more time for the things you cherish most.

Unlike traditional income derived from active employment, passive income allows you to break free from the constraints of trading your time for money. It's the money that works for you, not the other way around. As your passive income streams grow, they begin to cover your expenses, provide financial security, and eventually, enable you to live life on your own terms. This newfound financial freedom grants you the flexibility to pursue your passions, spend more time with loved ones, and seize opportunities without being tied to a nine-to-five job. It's the bridge to a life where you have control over your financial destiny, and passive income is the vehicle that can take you there.

Creating Passive Income Streams

The pursuit of passive income involves building financial assets that generate ongoing income without requiring your daily involvement. While this may take time and effort upfront, the ultimate goal is to secure a future where you can enjoy financial freedom and independence.

One fundamental step in creating passive income streams is to assess your skills and interests. By identifying your strengths and passions, you can uncover potential opportunities for generating passive income. This might involve creating digital products, such as online courses, or software applications, that can be sold repeatedly without ongoing effort. Alternatively, you could explore dividend-paying stocks or real estate investments that provide regular income with relatively little active participation. By leveraging your unique skills and interests, you can find passive income opportunities that align with your expertise and passions.

Examples:

- Real Estate Investment: Consider investing in rental properties or real estate investment trusts (REITs) to generate rental income or dividends.

- Invest in Dividend Stocks: Build a portfolio of dividend-paying stocks from reputable companies to receive regular dividend payments.

- Automated Online Businesses: Explore online business opportunities like e-commerce stores or affiliate marketing that can run with minimal day-to-day involvement.

- Create Intellectual Property: If you have creative skills, explore opportunities to create intellectual property that can generate royalties.

Practical Steps

Sometimes, the most challenging aspect of building passive income is simply knowing where to begin. The world of passive income streams can be vast and varied, which can be both exciting and overwhelming. However, by taking the first step and exploring the opportunities that align with your interests, skills, and resources, you can embark on a path that leads to greater financial independence and the flexibility to design the life you desire.

1. **Identify Your Niche**: Start by pinpointing an area or field where you have expertise or a strong interest. This could be real estate, stocks, online businesses, or other investment opportunities.

2. **Research and Plan**: Thoroughly research your chosen niche. Understand the market, potential returns, and associated risks. Develop a detailed plan to guide you.

3. **Invest Wisely**: Use your knowledge to invest in assets or opportunities that have the potential to generate passive income

4. **Diversify Your Income Streams**: Consider spreading your passive income sources to reduce risk and enhance stability.

5. **Monitor and Adjust**: Regularly assess the performance of your passive income streams and make adjustments as needed to maximize your earnings. This includes cashing out if necessary.

Conclusion

Passive income is the bridge that can lead you from financial dependence to financial freedom. By understanding the concept, identifying your passive income goals, diversifying your income streams, and monitoring your progress, you can gradually build a portfolio of passive income sources that work for you, allowing you to enjoy a life of greater financial security and flexibility. Remember, financial freedom is not an overnight achievement but a journey that starts with the first step towards passive income.

Furthermore, as you venture into the realm of passive income, it's essential to maintain a proactive mindset. Continuously seek new opportunities to grow your passive income streams and stay adaptable in the face of changing financial landscapes. Remember that your financial journey is dynamic, and new opportunities may arise along the way. Embrace the process, and with dedication and creativity, you can pave a path to lasting financial independence.

CHAPTER EIGHT

HABITS FOR FINANCIAL SUCCESS

Habits are deeply ingrained behaviors that often occur without conscious thought. The human brain is remarkably efficient in forming and executing habits. It does so by relying on a neural loop that consists of three key components: the cue, the routine, and the reward. The cue triggers the habit, the routine is the behavior itself, and the reward reinforces the habit by providing a sense of pleasure or satisfaction. Over time, the brain streamlines these processes, making habits increasingly automatic.

Contrary to the popular notion that it takes 21 days to form a habit, research suggests that the time required for habit formation varies widely. On average, it takes about 66 days to establish a new habit, but this can range from 18 days to 254 days depending on the individual and the complexity of the habit. Realistically, starting with small, manageable changes is the most effective way to develop new habits. Consistency is key; repeating the behavior at the same time and in the same context can help establish and reinforce habits. Gradual progression and positive reinforcement also contribute to habit formation. By understanding the science behind habits and employing practical techniques, individuals can deliberately shape their behaviors and transform their financial and personal lives.

Habits That Foster Financial Success

Habits play a pivotal role in determining your financial success. Just as a ship is guided by its daily charted course, your financial journey is shaped by the habits you cultivate. Consistent and well-considered financial habits, such as budgeting, saving, and prudent investment, can lead to long-term prosperity. On the contrary, poor financial habits, like impulsive spending or neglecting savings, can steer you off course. Recognizing the power of these habits is the first step to harnessing them to your advantage, making informed choices, and steering your financial ship toward the shores of success and stability.

We'll revisit some of the core concepts from Chapter Two and go deeper into transforming these ideas into ingrained financial habits.

- Budgeting: Cultivate the habit of budgeting. It helps you track your spending, identify areas for improvement, and make informed financial decisions. Make this a monthly habit. Layout your income and expenses for every month.

- Saving: Make saving a non-negotiable habit. Automatically allocate a portion of your income to savings before spending on discretionary items. The easiest way to do this is to include what is going into your savings in your budget.

- <u>Investing</u>: Develop the habit of regular investing. Consistent contributions to investment accounts can lead to long-term wealth growth.

- <u>Goal Setting</u>: Set clear financial goals and regularly review and adjust them. Goals give you a sense of direction and motivation.

- <u>Delayed Gratification</u>: Practice delayed gratification by postponing impulse purchases and focusing on long-term financial priorities. Remember we talked about the 30 day rule in Chapter 3. Apply that idea anytime you have the urge to make a purchase that is not an asset or necessity.

- <u>Continuous Learning</u>: Stay curious and informed about financial matters. Reading books, attending workshops, and seeking advice from experts can expand your financial knowledge.

Learn to Cue the Habit

Cues are important in the formation and execution of habits. They act as triggers, prompting us to engage in specific behaviors. They can take various forms, often tied to our daily routines or environments. For instance, a regular monthly reminder on your calendar may serve as a cue to review your budget and ensure you're on track. Opening your bills can be a cue to examine your expenses and make timely payments. Some people find that setting a specific time, like right after breakfast, to check their investments serves as a consistent cue for maintaining their investment habit.

Moreover, life events and milestones can act as powerful cues. For instance, reaching a certain age might cue you to begin retirement planning or setting up a will. Major life changes, such as getting married, having a child, or buying a home, can serve as cues to adjust your financial habits to accommodate these transitions. Identifying cues that work for you and aligning them with your financial goals is a practical way to initiate and reinforce financial habits. Whether it's a time-based cue, an environmental cue, or a life event cue, these triggers can help you stay on track and create lasting, beneficial financial habits.

The "Cue, Routine, Reward" framework helps understand how habits are triggered, what actions are taken, and the rewards received upon completing the routine. It's a practical way to visualize habit formation and implementation

Habit	Cue	Routine	Reward
Budgeting	Monthly arrival of bills	Track spending and plan budget	Financial control and peace of mind
Saving	Paycheck deposit	Automatically allocate portion to savings	Growing financial security
Investing	Regular payday	Make consistent contributions to investment accounts	Long-term wealth growth
Goal Setting	Goal review time	Define and adjust financial objectives	Motivation and clarity
Delayed Gratification	Shopping impulse	Postpone purchase and prioritize necessities	Reduced impulse spending
Continuous Learning	Free time	Read financial books, attend workshops, seek expert advice	Expanding financial knowledge

Identify Challenges and Limitations

Identifying financial challenges and limitations is a crucial step on the path to financial well-being. Start by conducting a thorough self-assessment of your financial situation. This includes analyzing your income, expenses, debts, and financial goals. Identify any recurring obstacles, such as excessive debt, overspending, or a lack of savings. Once you've pinpointed these challenges, you can begin to counter them with a strategic plan. For instance, if excessive debt is a concern, you might explore debt consolidation or budgeting to accelerate your repayment. If overspending is an issue, consider implementing spending limits or creating a more detailed budget. The key is to approach these challenges with a proactive mindset, seeking solutions that align with your financial goals and aspirations.

Practical Steps

Creating strong financial habits is like constructing a sturdy bridge to your financial goals. To start building these habits, you'll first want to take a close look at your existing routines and identify areas where you can make improvements. This means assessing your current budgeting and spending patterns, recognizing areas where you tend to overspend, and pinpointing any financial challenges that may be holding you back.

1. **Create a Financial Plan**: Start by outlining your financial goals and creating a detailed plan. This plan should include a budget, savings targets, and a debt reduction strategy. All of these are things that we have already talked about in earlier chapters.

2. **Budget Regularly**: Track your income and expenses regularly to understand where your money goes. We have discussed this so much already in this book. This must be a habit that you do every single month.

3. **Reduce Unnecessary Expenses**: Identify areas in your budget where you can cut back on unnecessary spending. This could include dining out less, canceling unused subscriptions, or finding more cost-effective alternatives. Again, every month go over these when you make your budget and adjust your spending.

4. **Seek Financial Education**: Invest time in learning about personal finance. Books, courses, and online resources can provide valuable insights and knowledge. Make this a daily habit. Dedicate 20 minutes to an hour each day to reading or watching an online video.

Once you've identified the areas for improvement, you can begin implementing practical steps to reinforce your financial habits. This might involve setting up automated systems for saving, setting clear financial goals, and developing a monthly budget that aligns with your objectives. You can also create specific, actionable plans to address your financial challenges head-on. These practical steps, combined with consistency and determination, will serve as the pillars for constructing your financial success. Remember that building strong financial habits takes time, patience, and a commitment to your financial well-being, but the rewards are well worth the effort.

Conclusion

Your habits serve as the compass guiding your financial journey, steering you towards your desired destination. They are the practical tools that help you convert your aspirations into reality. These rituals are essential in your quest for success.

By cultivating a sense of consistency and discipline in your daily habits, you are strengthening your ability to navigate through life's challenges. It will help you develop the skills to navigate through ups and downs. IHabits serve as more than just daily routines; they become the foundational elements of your future, ensuring that you can withstand any adversity and chart a course to lasting stability.

CHAPTER NINE

NAVIGATING CHALLENGES & SETBACKS

Life's unpredictability means that financial challenges are not a matter of if, but when they'll come your way. You need to find ways of understanding and effectively navigating these inevitable setbacks that you may encounter.

Financial challenges can manifest in various forms, including unexpected expenses, job loss, market downturns, or personal emergencies. These obstacles can disrupt your financial stability and lead to stress and uncertainty.

Examples

- <u>Sudden Medical Expenses</u>: Unexpected health issues can lead to substantial medical bills, impacting your financial well-being.

- <u>Job Loss</u>: A sudden termination or loss of income can pose a significant financial challenge.

- <u>Market Downturn:</u> A decline in the stock market can negatively affect investments and retirement accounts.

- <u>Emergency Repairs</u>: Urgent repairs to your home or vehicle can strain your budget.

- <u>Legal Matters</u>: Legal issues, such as lawsuits or legal fees, can be financially draining.

- <u>Natural Disasters</u>: Damage caused by natural disasters may result in unexpected expenses not covered by insurance.

- <u>Family Obligations</u>: Unexpected financial responsibilities, like supporting family members or paying for education, can arise.

- <u>Identity Theft</u>: Dealing with identity theft can lead to financial difficulties and legal expenses.

Resilience and Adaptation

The ability to bounce back is a vital trait for any type of success. It empowers you to face challenges head-on and adapt to unexpected circumstances. In this book, we've equipped you with a diverse array of financial principles, practical steps, and habits that are specifically designed to help you navigate whatever life throws your way. While challenges are inevitable, they are not insurmountable. Developing resilience means learning to respond effectively when faced with adversity.

Remember, resilience is not just about bouncing back but also about moving forward with greater strength and wisdom. Your Emergency Fund, one of the tools we've discussed in this book, plays a pivotal role in providing that safety net. Concepts such as budgeting, saving, and debt management offer foundational support. With all of these tools you're better prepared to weather the storms and come out on the other side stronger and more resilient than ever before.

Psychological Resilience

Resilience is often the key to turning simple ideas into meaningful, long-lasting habits. While the concepts we've discussed in this book may seem straightforward, the execution can be far from easy. The real challenge often lies within our minds and our ability to consistently apply these principles. The power of these financial habits lies not just in their simplicity but in their capacity to shape our financial well-being. It's the consistent, daily application of these principles that can lead to significant positive change in your financial life.

The struggle to build financial resilience and develop lasting habits is not to be underestimated. Your mind is your most powerful tool, but it can also be your greatest adversary. It's easy to revert to old behaviors or lose sight of your goals when faced with adversity or temptation. The journey to financial success is a mental battle as much as a financial one. Staying the course and maintaining a resilient mindset requires effort, self-awareness, and continuous practice. As you face financial challenges, remember that every obstacle presents an opportunity to test and reinforce your psychological resilience. It's these challenges that will ultimately shape your financial character and determine your path to success.

Practical Steps

Characteristics of psychological resilience can help you navigate financial challenges with a positive and empowered mindset.

1. **Focus on Solutions**: Cultivate a positive outlook and focus on solutions rather than dwelling on problems. Ruminating on the things that are wrong will not help you make them right.

2. **Emergency Fund:** Remember this? Maintain an emergency fund to cover unexpected expenses or income disruptions. Having three to six months' worth of living expenses set aside can provide a safety net during challenging times.

3. **Adaptability:** Be flexible and open to change, adjusting your financial plans when circumstances demand it. You might have to adjust your budget and do without some monthly subscriptions for a few months.

Conclusion

Financial challenges and setbacks are an inherent aspect of your financial path. It's essential to understand that these challenges don't dictate your financial future. By enhancing your resilience using tools like emergency funds, budget adjustments, and fostering psychological strength, you can conquer financial obstacles and maintain your trajectory towards financial success. Setbacks often serve as opportunities for increased financial knowledge and personal growth, ensuring that each hurdle you surmount brings you nearer to your financial objectives.

TIME OUT : REFLECT & REFOCUS

Congratulations on your journey through the chapters on Passive Income Streams, Habits, and Navigating Challenges. These topics are instrumental in your pursuit of financial success, and your commitment to learning and growing is commendable. As you pause for a moment of reflection, consider some questions and thoughts to help you refocus on your path.

Use this time to reflect on these questions and any other thoughts that come to mind. Remember that small, consistent steps can lead to significant financial growth. Your commitment to self-improvement and financial well-being is the driving force behind your continued success.

What Excites You?

Think about passive income stream ideas. Are there any that interest you? Any that you want to learn more about?

Financial Habits

Look at the financial habits you currently possess. Which habits have been serving you well, and which ones may need improvement? Consider the practical steps we've discussed and how you can implement them in your daily life.

Revisit Challenges

In the face of financial challenges, how have you displayed resilience? What strategies have you employed to bounce back and adapt effectively? Reflect on the tools and habits you've learned to navigate setbacks. Then remember a time or two when you responded poorly. Think of how you could respond better in the future.

Goals and Aspirations

Have they evolved or changed throughout your reading journey? Take some time to reevaluate and ensure your goals align with your newfound knowledge. Do you want to be out of debt? Save a down payment to purchase a house? If it helps you focus, write them down in a journal or somewhere.

Knowledge and Action

Knowledge without action yields no results. As you move forward, how will you apply the insights gained from these chapters into tangible financial changes in your life? What will be your first steps?

CELEBRATE

Take a moment to celebrate your commitment to financial growth and the steps you've taken. Every choice you make to enhance your financial well-being is a cause for celebration.

"The best time to plant a tree was 20 years ago. The second best time is now."

- Chinese Proverb

CHAPTER TEN

GIVING BACK & LEAVING A FINANCIAL LEGACY

Let's shift our focus from wealth accumulation to the meaningful impact we can have on the world. Giving back and leaving a financial legacy is not just about accumulating wealth; it's about using that wealth to make a positive difference in the lives of others and future generations.

As we embrace the idea of giving back, it's essential to consider the various ways you can leave a lasting imprint. Charitable giving is one avenue to explore, enabling you to support causes and organizations that align with your values. Whether it's supporting education, healthcare, environmental preservation, or community development, your financial resources can play a pivotal role in creating a brighter future for countless individuals. Beyond monetary contributions, your time and expertise can also leave a significant impact. Volunteering, mentoring, and sharing your knowledge can empower others to reach their full potential, extending your influence far beyond your financial contributions.

The Power of Generosity

Generosity is a transformative power that not only instigates lasting change but also fulfills your sense of purpose. It revolves around acknowledging the privilege that financial stability provides and channeling that privilege to make a meaningful impact in the lives of others. By extending a helping hand, you can not only influence the world around you but also experience a profound sense of personal fulfillment. Your generosity has the potential to become a legacy of compassion and positive change, a testament to the impact of your financial journey.

Ways to Give Back and Leave a Legacy

- <u>Volunteering</u>: While money is a valuable resource, your time and skills are equally precious. Volunteering can make a meaningful difference in your community or in the lives of others. Plus if you recall from earlier in the book money is actually time. Therefore, donating your time is sometimes just as good as donating your cash.

- <u>Charitable Donations</u>: Donating to causes or organizations that align with your values. Whether it's education, healthcare, the environment, or poverty alleviation, your contributions can make a significant impact.

- <u>Estate Planning</u>: In your estate plan, you can designate charitable beneficiaries, ensuring that a portion of your assets goes to causes you care about.

- <u>Philanthropic Foundations</u>: Establishing or contributing to a foundation allows you to create a structured approach to giving back. It can have a long-lasting impact and support a specific mission.

Practical Steps

Giving back and creating a financial legacy is deeply personal, and the steps you take should align with your unique values and goals.

1. **Create a Giving Plan:** Develop a structured plan for your charitable activities. Establish a timeline for contributing to causes you care about and work your donations into your monthly budget.

2. **Educate Yourself:** Research charitable organizations and initiatives to ensure your donations are aligned with your goals. Understand their missions, financial transparency, and the impact they make.

3. **Document Your Legacy:** Create a will or legacy plan that clearly outlines how your assets will be distributed to charitable causes. This ensures your philanthropic intentions are carried out after your passing.

Conclusion

Engaging in philanthropy and crafting a financial legacy represents the pinnacle of your financial endeavors. It signifies an understanding that wealth holds a purpose beyond individual gain and can serve to improve the world. By introspectively aligning with your values, formulating a structured philanthropic plan, and actively engaging your loved ones, you can harness your financial resources to establish an enduring legacy that transcends your lifetime. In this ultimate section, you hold the power not only to safeguard your financial future but to imprint a legacy that leaves a long-lasting, meaningful mark on the lives of others, ensuring that your financial success resonates far into the future.

JUST BE BETTER

As we conclude our journey through these pages, it's essential to revisit some key takeaways that have the power to transform your financial life. First and foremost, remember the profound impact of your mindset. The way you perceive and interact with money shapes the entire landscape of your financial journey. Be mindful of how you view wealth, whether it's as a means to an end or a tool to create a better life. Always bear in mind that money isn't just currency; it's a measurement of your life force – your time, your energy. Each dollar represents a portion of your existence, so choose how you spend it wisely.

A cornerstone of this transformative path lies in cultivating strong financial habits. One such habit is the monthly budget. It may sound simple, yet it is the bedrock of financial stability, allowing you to set intentions for your money, rather than having your spending dictate your life. Practice the 30-day rule to curb impulse spending. This technique empowers you to assess whether a purchase is truly necessary or merely a fleeting desire, leading you to more deliberate choices.

Our journey has unveiled the importance of nurturing the seeds of abundance, fostering psychological resilience, and embracing the art of giving back. Wealth is not solely about accumulating assets; it's about creating a legacy that enriches the lives of others. By employing these strategies, you have the potential to leave a lasting impact that transcends your lifetime.

As you reflect upon your adventure through the world of personal finance, remember that financial wisdom, like any other wisdom, is a path, not a destination. It is a lifelong journey that you can embrace with the knowledge that every step you take shapes your financial reality. Continue to learn, grow, and adapt because your financial success is not measured solely by the number of zeros in your bank account. It is measured by the peace of mind, the choices, and the life you lead.

The wisdom shared in these pages is designed to be revisited as you navigate the complexities of the financial world. Let it serve as a guiding light in moments of uncertainty and a reminder of the core principles when financial choices become convoluted. Your journey to financial well-being is ongoing, and I trust that you will use this knowledge to shape a brighter, more prosperous future for yourself and those you touch along the way.

BONUS : UNDERSTANDING COMPOUND INTEREST

Compound interest is a powerful financial concept that can significantly impact your retirement savings. It's like a magic trick that multiplies your money over time, and it's essential to grasp its mechanics for a secure financial future.

Essentially, compound interest means that your money earns interest on the interest it has already earned. It's a cycle of growth that accelerates over time. The more you save and invest, the more you benefit from this snowball effect.

Let's break it down with an example:

Suppose you invest $1,000 in an account with a 5% annual interest rate.

- After the first year, you'd earn $50 in interest, making your total balance $1,050.

- In the second year, you'd earn 5% interest on the new total, which is $1,050. This equals $52.50, raising your balance to $1,102.50.

- In the third year, your interest is calculated on the new balance, and so on.

As the years go by, the interest you earn becomes a more significant portion of your balance. This compounding effect can lead to substantial growth over time. The longer you leave your money invested, the more it multiplies.

Now, imagine applying this principle to your retirement savings. If you consistently contribute to your retirement accounts and allow them to grow over several decades, compound interest can work its magic, potentially turning your modest contributions into a substantial nest egg.

Remember, the key to harnessing compound interest is to start early and be consistent with your savings and investments. Over time, this simple concept can help you achieve your retirement goals and enjoy financial security in your later years.

This table shows how compound interest allows your initial investment to grow over the years. With each passing year, you earn interest not only on your original $1,000 but also on the interest you've previously earned. Over time, your total balance increases significantly, thanks to the power of compounding.

Year	Initial Investment	Annual Interest Rate (%)	Interest Earned	Total Balance
1	$1,000	5%	$50	$1,050
2	$1,050	5%	$52.50	$1,102.50
3	$1,102.50	5%	$55.13	$1,157.63
4	$1,157.63	5%	$57.88	$1,215.51
5	$1,215.51	5%	$60.78	$1,276.29
6	$1,276.29	5%	$63.81	$1,340.10

Now let's see what it looks like if you increase that initial investment at an annual interest rate of 8%.

Year	Initial Investment	Annual Interest (%)	Interest Earned	Total Balance
1	$10,000.00	8.00	$800.00	$10,800.00
2	$10,800.00	8.00	$864.00	$11,664.00
3	$11,664.00	8.00	$933.12	$12,597.12
4	$12,597.12	8.00	$1,007.77	$13,604.89
5	$13,604.89	8.00	$1,088.39	$14,693.28

BONUS : ACCELERATE YOUR MORTGAGE PAYOFF

Let's explore a strategy that can help you pay off your mortgage (or any loan) more quickly while minimizing the total interest paid. This approach involves making multiple payments per month, which can significantly reduce the loan term and total interest cost. The key is to leverage the power of compounding and consistent extra payments.

Look at the details of your loan, sometimes this isn't allowed and early payoff may be penalized by your bank.

Table: Mortgage Payoff Comparison

Here's a table that compares two scenarios: making monthly payments versus making bi-weekly payments (every two weeks). We'll use a hypothetical $200,000 mortgage with a 30-year term at a 4% interest rate for this illustration:

Payment Frequency	Monthly Payment	Bi-Weekly Payment	Total Payments	Loan Term	Total Interest Paid
Monthly Payments	$954.83	N/A	360	30 years	$143,739
Bi-Weekly Payments	N/A	$477.42	390	29.1 years	$132,525

Explanation:

1. *Monthly Payments*: With monthly payments, you pay approximately $954.83 each month. Over 30 years, you'll make a total of 360 payments and pay $143,739 in interest.

2. *Bi-Weekly Payments*: Making payments every two weeks, you'll pay approximately $477.42 each time. As there are 52 weeks in a year, you'll make 26 payments (equivalent to 13 monthly payments) in a year. This means you'll make 390 payments over approximately 29.1 years, and the total interest paid will be $132,525.

Key Takeaways:

- By making bi-weekly payments, you will make one extra payment each year (13 instead of 12).

- This additional payment reduces the loan balance more quickly and accelerates the payoff schedule.

- Over time, you save $11,214 in interest and pay off the loan approximately 10 months earlier with bi-weekly payments.

This strategy demonstrates how small, consistent changes in your payment frequency can make a substantial difference in the long run. Check with your lender to see if you are allowed to make extra payments on your loan.

WAIT!

Let's just dig a little deeper. What would it look like if you paid on your mortgage daily?

$200,000 mortgage with a 30-year term at a 4% interest rate when you make 30 payments each month, one for every day:

Payment Frequency	Monthly Payment	Total Payments	Loan Term	Total Interest Paid
Monthly Payments	$954.83	360	30 years	$143,739
Daily Payments	$66.22	10,950	7.5 years	$53,750

Explanation:

Daily Payments: With daily payments, you pay approximately $66.22 every day, resulting in a total of 10,950 payments over approximately 7.5 years. The total interest paid in this scenario is $53,750.

Key Takeaways:

- Making daily payments significantly reduces the loan term and total interest paid.

- This approach requires a high level of consistency, discipline, and the ability to make smaller daily payments.

- Over time, you save $90,989 in interest and pay off the loan more than 22 years earlier with daily payments compared to the traditional monthly payment schedule.

Consider this comparison to understand the impact of payment frequency on the mortgage term and total interest paid. Choose a payment strategy that best aligns with you financial capabilities and goals and one that your bank will allow.

THE END

"If you know the way broadly you
will see it in everything."

- Miyamoto Musashi

83600455R00066